Nita Mehta's
Punjabi
Cooking

Nita Mehta

B.Sc. (Home Science), M.Sc. (Food and Nutrition), Gold Medalist

SNAB
Publishers Pvt Ltd

Nita Mehta's
Punjabi
Cooking

© Copyright 2002-2005 **SNAB** Publishers Pvt Ltd

3rd Print 2005
ISBN 81-7869-030-6

Food Styling and Photography: **SNAB**

Layout and laser typesetting :

National Information Technology Academy
3A/3, Asaf Ali Road
New Delhi-110002
N.I.T.A. ☎ 23252948

Published by :

SNAB
Publishers Pvt. Ltd.
3A/3 Asaf Ali Road,
New Delhi - 110002
Tel : 23252948, 23250091
Telefax:91-11-23250091

Editorial and Marketing office:
E-159, Greater Kailash-II, N.Delhi-48
*Fax:*91-11-29225218, 29229558
*Tel:*91-11-29214011, 29218727, 29218574
E-Mail: nitamehta@email.com
✉ snab@snabindia.com
*Website:*http://www.nitamehta.com
Website: http://www.snabindia.com

Distributed by :

THE VARIETY BOOK DEPOT
A.V.G. Bhavan, M 3 Con Circus,
New Delhi - 110 001
Tel : 23417175, 23412567; Fax : 23415335
Email: varietybookdepot@rediffmail.com

Printed by :
PRESS TECH.

Rs. 89/-

Introduction

*P*unjab is a land of healthy, fun loving, robust people. They have hearty appetites and enjoy good food.

They enjoy non-vegetarian food as well as the vegetables equally. In fact many of their meat preparations are with vegetables such as *Methi Chicken* and *Saag Meat*. The Punjabi snacks like *"Besan Di Murgi"* is a delightful fennel flavoured fried chicken coated with gramflour. The special *Achaari Paneer Tikka* is a hot favourite.

The book also includes the delicious paranthas of Punjab as well as the milk based rabri, kheer and kulfi to complete the meal.

After these recipes, you are bound to say – "Punjab Da Jawab Nahi"!

Nita Mehta

Contents

Introduction   5

CHICKEN, MUTTON, FISH   9

Raarha Meat   10

Butter Chicken   12

Nimbu Waali Machhi   15

Lamb Tikka Masala   16

Achaari Murg   18

Surkh Kukkad   21

Meat Khadha Masala   22

Taya ji Di Machhi   24

Kofta Curry   26

Kadhai Chicken   28

Methi Chicken   30

Dahiwala Mutton   32

Tomato Fish   34

Kasoori Murg Malai   36

VEGETABLES & DALS 39

Palak Malai Kofta   40
Baingan Di Kachri   43
Saabut Gobhi   44
Pindi Chhole   46
Lahori Malai Kofte   49
Paneer Makhani   52
Matar Khumb Curry   54

Sarson Da Saag   56
Paneer Taka-Tak   59
Punj Rattani Dal   62
Dal Makhani (Maanh Sabat)   64
Achaari Baingans   66
Khaja Aloo   68

SNACKS   70

VEGETARIAN

Punjabi Aloo Tikki   73
Achaari Paneer Tikka   84

NON-VEGETARIAN

Besan Di Murgi   71
Amritsari Machhi   76
Mewa Kebab   78
Chicken Lollipops   80
Fried Fish   82

7

ROTI & CHAAWAL   86

VEGETARIAN
Bhature   87
Makki Di Roti   88
Poodina Parantha   89
Amritsari Nan   92
Peethi Poori   94

NON-VEGETARIAN
Champae Waale Chaawal   90

MITTHA   95

Pista Kesar Kulfi   96
Jalebi Te Rabri   97

Kesari Mitthe Chaawal   100
Chhuare Te Chaawal Di Kheer   102

CHICKEN, MUTTON, FISH

Raarha Meat

The name basically indicates a masala mutton dish that has been well fried.

Serves 2-3

250 gms mutton
¾ cup curd - beaten well till smooth
1 tsp salt
5 tbsp ghee/oil
1" stick dalchini (cinnamon)
2 moti illaichi (black cardamoms)
1 tej patta (bay leaf)
1 big onion - finely chopped (1 cup)
1 tsp ginger paste
1 tsp garlic paste
1 big tomato - finely chopped (1 cup)
½ tsp haldi powder, ¾ tsp garam masala powder
1 tsp red chilli powder

GARNISHING
some fresh chopped dhania leaves

1. Whisk curd. Add salt and mutton and let it marinate for 1-1½ hours.
2. Heat ghee/oil in a pressure cooker.
3. Add dalchini, illaichi and tej patta. Fry for few seconds.
4. Add onion. Fry till light brown.
5. Add ginger and garlic paste, haldi, garam masala, red chilli powder and tomatoes. Cook till tomatoes are soft and well mixed.
6. Add mutton along with the marinade and cook till oil separates.
7. Add ¾ cup water. Mix well. Close the cooker and give 1-2 whistles. Keep on low heat for 15 minutes. Remove from fire.
8. When pressure drops, open cooker and again fry till oil/ghee separates. Sprinkle fresh dhania on top and serve hot with rotis.

Butter Chicken

The all time favourite! Tandoori chicken in makhani gravy. Use degi mirch for a bright colour of the gravy.

Serves 4

1 chicken (800 gms) - cut into 12 pieces

FOR TANDOORI CHICKEN
2 tbsp lemon juice, ½ tsp chilli powder, 1¼ tsp salt, or to taste
½ cup thick hung curd (hang 1 cup curd)
2 tbsp thick malai or 2 tbsp cream, 1 tbsp garlic paste, 1 tsp ginger paste
½ tsp kala namak, 1 tsp garam masala, 1 tsp tandoori masala or chaat masala
few drops orange red colour

MAKHANI GRAVY
2 tbsp butter, 2-3 tbsp oil
1 tej patta (bay leaf)
2 tbsp ginger-garlic paste
½ kg (6-7) tomatoes - blended to a very smooth puree

½ tsp kashmiri or degi mirch, ¼ tsp sugar or to taste, salt to taste
1 cup milk, 2-4 tbsp cream
3 tbsp cashewnuts - soaked in hot water for 15 minutes & ground to a very fine paste with a little water
½ tsp garam masala, 1 tsp tandoori masala, 2 tsp kasoori methi

1. Wash, pat dry chicken. Make incisions on breast, thighs and drumsticks.
2. Rub lemon juice, salt & chilli pd on chicken. Keep aside for ½ hour.
3. Mix curd, malai, garlic and ginger paste, kala namak, garam masala, tandoori masala and colour. Rub the chicken with this mixture. Keep aside for 3-4 hours in the fridge.
4. Heat the gas tandoor on moderate flame or an oven to 180°C. Place the chicken on the grill or wire rack (in the oven place a tray underneath the chicken to collect the drippings).
5. Grill for 15 minutes. Brush pieces with oil or pour some oil with a spoon on all the pieces. Turn pieces and grill for another 10-15 minutes, till the chicken is dry and well cooked. Be careful not to make the chicken blackish and burnt. Keep tandoori chicken aside.
6. To prepare the makhani gravy, heat butter and oil together in non

contd...

stick pan. Add tej patta. Stir for a few seconds. Add ginger and garlic paste, cook until liquid evaporates and paste just changes colour.

7. Add pureed tomatoes, degi mirch and sugar. Cook until the puree turns very dry and fat separates. Add salt to taste.

8. Add cashew paste, stir for 2 minutes on medium heat. Remove from fire and cool for 15-20 minutes.

9. After the tomato masala cools completely, add 1 cup milk and about ½ cup of water to get the desired consistency of the gravy. Return to fire. Keeping on low heat, bring to a boil, stirring constantly.

10. Add chicken. Simmer for 2 minutes till the gravy turns to a bright colour. Remove from fire and stir in cream, stirring continuously. Add garam masala, kasoori methi and tandoori masala. Stir. Remove from fire. Garnish with 1 tbsp of fresh cream, slit green chillies and coriander.

Note: Instead of cooking the chicken in the tandoor, you can marinate chicken, and then cook in a non stick pan or kadhai instead of a tandoor. For that, add chicken pieces to some hot oil. Stir fry on high flame till the chicken is brown and crisp. Lower heat, cover and cook for 5 minutes till chicken is tender. Put in the gravy.

Nimbu Waali Machhi

A simple but delicious fish with the prominent flavour of pepper and lemon. Can be served as a snack too.

Serves 2-3

400 gms fish (5-6 pieces) - preferably boneless and skinless
6 tbsp lemon juice, 1 tsp salt, 3 tsp pepper - preferably freshly ground
2 tsp garlic paste, 2 tsp ginger paste
some cornflour for rolling (coating), oil for frying

1. Rub fish with 1 tsp salt, 2 tbsp besan and 1 tbsp lemon juice. Wash well to remove any smell.
2. Mix together 6 tbsp lemon juice, 1 tsp salt, 3 tsp freshly ground pepper, ginger and garlic paste. Rub this on the fish and let it marinate for 2-3 hours in the fridge.
3. Heat oil. Roll each piece of fish in dry cornflour so that the cornflour coats the fish lightly. Deep fry till cooked and crisp. Serve hot with chutney/sauce garnished with lemon wedges.

Lamb Tikka Masala

Dry mutton tikka coated with thick masala.

Picture on backcover   *Serves 4*

250 gms mutton (boneless) - cut into 2" pieces

MARINADE

1 tbsp lemon juice, 3 tbsp ginger - garlic paste
1 cup thick curd - tie in a muslin cloth & hang for 1 hour
1 tbsp raw papaya paste (kachha papita) -peel, deseed and blend in a blender or
1 tbsp kachri powder, ¼ tsp soda-bicarbonate (mitha soda)
2 onions - cut into slices, deep fried till golden and ground to a paste
½ tsp green cardamom powder (chhoti illaichi), 1 tsp salt, 1 tsp pepper powder

MASALA

2 tbsp oil, ¼ tsp sarson (mustard seeds), ½ tsp kalonji (black onion seeds)
1 onion - sliced, 2 tomatoes - chopped, 2 green chillies - finely chopped
½ cup coconut milk, ½ tsp salt, or to taste
2 tbsp mint leaves (poodina) - finely chopped, 2 tbsp coriander - finely chopped
1½ tbsp lemon juice, ½ tsp garam masala

1. Wash and pat dry the mutton pieces. Prick them with a fork. Mix all the ingredients of the marinade with the mutton. Let the mutton marinate for atleast 4 hours or even more in the refrigerator. To cook the botis, remove from fridge and let them come to room temperature. Heat an electric oven at 150°C or a gas tandoor on moderate flame. Thread 5 to 6 pieces of mutton onto each greased skewer or place the botis on a greased wire rack of the oven. Rub with the left over marinade.

2. Grill for 15- 20 minutes turning them 2 to 3 times inbetween. When slightly dry, spoon or brush some (about 2 tbsp) oil on them. Cook for another 10 minutes or till done. Remove the tikkas from the skewer.

3. For the masala, heat 2 tbsp oil. Add mustard seeds and kalonji.

4. Wait for a minute. Add onions and garlic. Saute over medium heat until onions turn golden brown. Add tomatoes and chopped green chillies. Cook till oil separates. Add coconut milk and salt. Bring to a boil, stirring continuously. Lower heat and cook for 5 minutes or until masala turns thick.

5. To serve, add cooked mutton tikka to the masala. Add mint, coriander, lemon juice and garam masala. Mix well and serve hot.

Achaari Murg

Picture on facing page   *Serves 5-6*

1 chicken (800 gm) - cut into 12 pieces
10 tbsp mustard oil
2 large onions - chopped finely or grated
2 tbsp ginger paste
2 tbsp garlic paste
1 tsp haldi powder, 2 tsp salt
2 tsp sugar, 2 tsp red chilli powder (Kashmiri)
1 cup curd - well beaten
4 tbsp lemon juice
some fresh dhania for garnishing

COLLECT TOGETHER
8-10 laung (cloves), 5-6 chhoti illaichi (green cardamoms)
1 tsp shah jeera (black cumin), 1 tsp methi dana (fenugreek seeds)
½ tsp kalaunji (onion seeds), 2 tsp rai (mustard seeds)
a pinch of hing (asafoetida), 5-6 whole, dry red chillies

Punjabi Cooking

1. Heat mustard oil till it smokes. Remove from fire and cool.
2. Heat oil again. Add all the collected spices - laung, chhoti illaichi, shah jeera, methi dana, kalaunji, rai, hing and whole, dry red chillies. Fry for ½ minute till methi dana turns golden.
3. Add onions and fry till golden brown.
4. Add ginger and garlic paste. Fry for 1-2 minutes.
5. Add chicken, salt, haldi, sugar and red chilli powder. Fry for 3-4 minutes on high flame.
6. Reduce heat. Add well beaten curd. Keep stirring till it boils. Cook, stirring all the time for another 2 minutes.
7. Cover and cook on low heat for 12 minutes or till chicken is tender.
8. Add lemon juice. Give 1-2 boils. Add ¼ cup water if you like and give 2-3 boils.
9. Serve hot, garnished with fresh dhania.

Note: Paneer or Dum aloo made in this way is also very delicious.

Surkh Kukkad

Use Kashmiri chillies to get a bright red coloured dry chicken.

Serves 5-6

1 chicken (800 gm) - cut into 12 pieces or pieces of your choice
1½ tsp garlic paste, 1½ tsp ginger paste, 2 large tomatoes - finely chopped
1½ tsp salt, 1½ tsp dhania powder, 1 tsp garam masala powder
6-7 tbsp oil/ghee

RED CHILLI-ONION PASTE (GRIND TOGETHER)
15-20 dried, whole Kashmiri chillies - deseeded and soaked in water for ½ hour
2 medium sized onions

1. Heat oil. Add ground red chilli-onion paste and ginger and garlic pastes. Fry well till the onion turns golden brown and leaves oil.
2. Add tomatoes and fry till they turn pulpy and get well mixed.
3. Add chicken, salt, dhania powder and garam masala. Mix. Stir fry for 3-4 minutes. Lower heat. Cover tightly and cook for 10-12 minutes or till chicken is tender. Sprinkle water in between if required. Serve.

Meat Khadha Masala

Picture on cover   *Serves 6-8*

1 kg mutton
¾ cup ghee
4 onions - chopped
5 tbsp garlic - chopped, 5 tbsp ginger - chopped, 5 green chillies - chopped
4 tomatoes - chopped, 2 cups yogurt - beat till smooth, 2 tsp salt or to taste

KHADHA MASALAS
2 moti illaichi (black cardamoms), 5-6 chhoti illaichi (green cardamoms)
5-6 laung (cloves), 1" stick dalchini (cinnamon)
1 tej patta (bay leaf), 2-3 blades javetri (mace)

CRUSHED OR POUNDED MASALAS
2 tsp saboot dhania (coriander seeds) - pounded or crushed coarsely
3-4 whole red chillies - pounded or crushed coarsely
10-15 saboot kali mirch (peppercorns) - pounded
1 tsp shah jeera (black cumin) - powdered

1. Heat ghee in a pressure cooker. Collect all khadha masalas together and add to hot oil. Saute over medium heat for a minute till it begins to crackle.
2. Add onions and cook till golden brown. Add garlic, ginger and green chillies. Stir for a few minutes.
3. Add mutton pieces and the pounded spices.
4. Bhuno till the mutton pieces are brown, for about 7-8 minutes.
5. Lower the heat add the yogurt and bhuno for 5-10 minutes.
6. Add the tomatoes and salt. Bhuno till the masala leaves ghee.
7. Add 2½ cups of water and preesure cook for 7 minutes on high flame when pressure forms and then for 5 minutes on low flame. Remove from fire and let the pressure drop by itself.
8. Sprinkle garam masala and coriander.
9. Garnish with slit green chillies. Serve with naan or parantha.

Taya ji Di Machhi

One of my uncle makes this fish. It is delicious and in our family it is called uncle's fish. This can be served as a snack or with the main meal.

Serves 4-5

400 gms fish (Singhara or any other fish of your choice) - preferably boneless and skinless, cut into medium size pieces
mustard oil for frying
fresh coriander leaves and lemon wedges for garnishing

MIX TOGETHER
2 eggs - beaten lightly
2 tbsp fresh coriander leaves - finely chopped
2 tsp garlic paste
1¼ tsp salt
1½ tsp Kashmiri red chilli powder (adjust to taste)
½ tsp dhania powder
½ tsp amchoor powder (increase to 1 tsp if you prefer a sour taste)
½ tsp garam masala

1. Rub fish pieces with 1 tsp salt, 2 tbsp besan and juice of 1 lemon. Wash well and pat dry.
2. Beat eggs lightly. Add fresh coriander, garlic paste, salt, red chilli powder, dhania powder, amchoor powder and garam masala powder. Mix well.
3. Add fish pieces and mix well so that fish is well coated with the mixture. Leave to marinate for 2-3 hours in the fridge.
4. Heat mustard oil. Pick up the fish pieces, leaving the extra marinade behind. Fry to a golden colour. Keep fish aside.
5. Heat a non stick frying pan. Add 1-2 tbsp mustard oil and swirl it around so that the bottom of the pan is coated with the oil.
6. Add fried fish pieces to the pan and pour all the remaining marinade on the fish. Cover and cook on low heat for 5-6 minutes, overturning the pieces once or twice to ensure even heating.
7. Serve hot garnished with fresh coriander leaves and lemon wedges.

Kofta Curry

Serves 10-12

400 gms keema - wash and squeeze out all the water and grind well in the mixer
1" piece ginger - chopped, 4 flakes garlic - chopped
1 egg
1 tsp red chilli powder (Kashmiri), 1½ tsp salt, 1 tsp garam masala

GRAVY
4 medium onions, 1½" piece ginger, 6 flakes garlic
5-6 moti illaichi (black cardamoms), 2 tej patta (bay leaves)
1½" stick dalchini (cinnamon), 5-6 laung (cloves)
2 tsp red chilli powder (Kashmiri), 2 tsp salt, ½ tsp haldi
1 tsp dhania powder, 1 tsp jeera powder, 1 tsp garam masala
4 tomatoes - pureed in the mixer
12 tbsp curd
7 tbsp oil plus 3 tbsp pure ghee or 10 tbsp oil

1. Wash keema well and squeeze out all the water by placing it in a strainer and pressing it.

2. Grind the keema along with ginger and garlic to a fine paste.
3. Remove from mixer. Add egg, salt, garam masala and red chilli powder. Mix well. Form balls and keep aside.
4. For the gravy, grind together onions, ginger and garlic to a fine paste.
5. Heat oil and ghee. Add khada garam masalas - moti illaichi, dalchini, laung and tej patta and fry for 1 minute.
6. Add ground onions and fry well till it turns dark brown.
7. Add pureed tomatoes. Mix and add masalas - red chilli, salt, haldi, dhania, jeera and garam masala. Cook till tomatoes turn dry.
8. Add well beaten curd and keep stirring till oil separates.
9. Add 3 cups of water. Give a boil. To the boiling gravy, one by one add the keema balls. Do not stir. Give 2-3 boils.
10. Lower heat. Cover and let them cook for 25-30 minutes or till the koftas turn soft. Garnish with fresh dhania and serve.

Note: For egg curry, instead of keema koftas, add full boiled eggs. They should be added towards the end and the amount of water reduced to 1½ cups. Let the gravy simmer for 15 minutes before adding eggs. Simmer for another 5-7 minutes and serve.

Kadhai Chicken

A tomato based chicken, flavoured with fenugreek and coriander.

Picture on page 1   *Serves 6*

1 medium sized (800 gms) chicken - cut into 8 or 12 pieces
7 tbsp oil
¼ tsp methi dana (fenugreek seeds)
1 onion - cut into slices
15-20 flakes garlic - crushed to a paste (3 tsp)
6 large (750 gm) tomatoes - chopped
2 tbsp chopped ginger, 2-3 green chillies - chopped
½ cup chopped green coriander
½ cup tomato puree
2 tsp salt, or to taste, 1 tsp red chilli powder, 1 tsp garam masala
1 tbsp kasoori methi
2 capsicums - cut into fingers
1" piece ginger - cut into match sticks, 1-2 green chillies - cut into thin slices
4-5 tbsp cream

CRUSH OR POUND TOGETHER
4-5 whole, dry red chillies
1 tbsp saboot dhania (coriander seeds)

1. Pound red chillies and saboot dhania on a chakla-belan (rolling board & pin) to crush roughly. Keep aside.
2. Heat oil in a kadhai. Reduce heat. Add methi dana. When it turns golden brown, add the pounded dhania and red chillies.
3. Stir for 30 seconds and add garlic paste. Stir for 30 seconds.
4. Add onion cook on medium heat till light golden.
5. Add tomatoes. Bring to a boil. Add chopped ginger and green chillies. Add coriander. Reduce heat and simmer for 5-7 minutes. Add salt.
6. Add chicken. Bhuno for 4-5 minutes on medium flame, stirring occasionally, until the oil leaves the masala and you get a thick masala gravy. Cover and cook for 10 minutes till tender, stirring occasionally.
7. Add tomato puree, red chilli powder, garam masala and kasoori methi. Stir for 2-3 minutes.
8. Add the capsicum, ginger match sticks & green chilli slices. Mix well.
9. Reduce heat. Add cream. Mix well and remove from fire. Serve hot.

Methi Chicken

Serves 5-6

1 chicken (800 gms) - cut into small pieces or use boneless pieces
4 cups finely chopped fresh methi leaves (fenugreek greens)
2 cups curd - well beaten
8-10 tbsp ghee/oil
2 large tomatoes - pureed in the mixer
2 tsp salt, 1½ tsp garam masala

GRIND TOGETHER TO A PASTE
2 large onions
3-4 green chillies (use according to taste)
1½" piece ginger
6-7 flakes garlic

TOPPING
3-4 tbsp ghee, ½ tsp red chilli powder

1.   Grind together onions, green chillies, garlic and ginger to a fine paste.
2.   Heat oil/ghee. Add onion paste and fry the paste to a rich brown colour.
3.   Add tomatoes, salt & garam masala. Cook till masala turns dry and oil separates.
4.   Add chicken and fry well for 5-6 minutes.
5.   Reduce heat. Add chopped methi and curd. Stir till it boils.
6.   Cook till dry. The chicken will get tender during this time, check if the chicken is not completely cooked, cover and keep on low heat for a few minutes till chicken turns tender.
7.   When the chicken turns dry and tender, transfer to a serving dish.
8.   Heat 4 tbsp ghee. Add red chilli powder. Remove from fire. Pour over the hot chicken. Serve immediately with nan.

Dahiwala Mutton

A quick but delicious dish with very little gravy - which can be dried completely also. Champae (ribs) can also be prepared in this manner and can be served as a snack.

Serves 2-3

MARINATE FOR 1-2 HOURS
250 gms mutton
1 cup curd
¾ tsp salt
¾ tsp red chilli powder (Kashmiri)
¾ tsp dhania powder

OTHER INGREDIENTS
5 tbsp oil/ghee
1 big onion - chopped (1 cup)
1 tsp garlic paste
1 tsp ginger paste

ADD AT THE END
¼ tsp garam masala and some kasoori methi
½-1 tbsp pure ghee, ¼ tsp red chilli powder

1. Mix together curd, salt, dhania powder and red chilli. Marinate mutton in this for 1-2 hours.
2. Heat oil/ghee in a cooker. Add chopped onions; ginger and garlic paste. Fry for 1-2 minutes.
3. Add mutton pieces without any extra marinade and fry for 5-7 minutes.
4. Add all the left over marinade. Mix well.
5. Add 1 cup water. Close the cooker and give 2-3 whistles. Keep on low heat for 15 minutes.
6. When pressure drops, add garam masala and kasoori methi. Mix well. Cook for 2-3 minutes, mixing all the time so that the onion gets minced and the masala gravy coats the mutton.
7. At the time of serving, heat ½-1 tbsp pure ghee. Add ¼ tsp red chilli powder. Cook for 1-2 seconds. Pour over hot mutton and serve.

Note: If you want a dry mutton, you can dry all the gravy.

Tomato Fish

Serves 4-5

500 gms fish - cut into 2"- 3" pieces (preferably boneless and skinless)
oil for frying

MARINADE
1 tsp salt
1 tsp red chilli powder
2 tbsp lemon juice
1 tsp dhania powder
1 tsp jeera powder

GRAVY
500 gms (6 medium) ripe red tomatoes - blanched (put in hot water and skin
removed) and then pureed till smooth
5-6 tbsp oil
1 tbsp garlic paste
1¼-1½ tsp red chilli powder (Kashmiri) - according to taste

1¼ tsp salt
1 tsp garam masala
1 tsp dhania powder
1½ tsp sugar
2 tbsp kasoori methi

1. Rub fish with a 1 tsp salt, 2 tbsp besan and juice of 1 lemon. Wash well to remove any smell.
2. Mix all ingredients given under marinade and marinate the fish in it for 10-15 minutes.
3. Heat oil and fry the fish lightly, a few pieces at a time. Do not make it crisp. Remove and keep aside.
4. For the gravy, blanch tomatoes by boiling whole tomatoes in water for 4-5 minutes. Remove skin and puree in a mixer to a smooth puree.
5. Heat 5-6 tbsp oil. Add garlic and fry till light brown.
6. Add tomato puree and all other seasonings including kasoori methi. Give one boil, stirring continuously.
7. Slide in the fish pieces and let them boil for 4-5 minutes.
8. Serve hot garnished with fresh dhania and green chillies.

Kasoori Murg Malai

Curd and cream form the base of this white gravy with a fragrant flavour of fenugreek.

Picture on facing page   Serves 5-6

1 chicken (800 gm) - cut into 12 pieces or 500 gm boneless - cut into 2" pieces
1 cup curd - hang for ½ hour and then beat till smooth
150 ml (1 cup) fresh cream
1 tbsp kasoori methi (dried fenugreek leaves)
6 tbsp oil
1 tsp garam masala
1½ tsp salt, or to taste
1 tsp white pepper (adjust to taste)

ONION PASTE (GRIND TOGETHER)
2 medium onions
6 flakes garlic, 1" piece ginger, 1-2 green chillies
2 tbsp water

Punjabi Cooking

1. Heat oil. Add onion paste and fry till it just starts to change colour. Do not make it brown as the gravy is whitish.
2. Add chicken, salt, garam masala and white pepper. Fry for 3-4 minutes on moderate heat till chicken changes colour.
3. Add hung curd and kasoori methi. Mix well and cook for 3-4 minutes.
4. Cover and cook on low heat for 15 minutes or till chicken is tender.
5. Add ½ cup water and bring to a boil. Simmer for 2-3 minutes to get a thick masala gravy.
6. Keeping the heat low, add fresh cream. Mix well and give one boil, stirring continuously on low heat.
7. Serve hot garnished with kasoori methi and fresh dhania.

VEGETABLES & DALS

Palak Malai Kofta

Picture on cover   *Serves 6-8*

KOFTAS (12-13)
100 gm paneer - mashed
2 slices bread - remove sides
3 tbsp curd
1/8 tsp baking powder
1 green chilli - chopped finely
1 tbsp finely chopped coriander
½ tsp salt & ½ tsp pepper, to taste
¼ tsp red chill powder
1½ tbsp maida (plain flour)
a few pieces of cashewnuts

PALAK GRAVY (BOIL TOGETHER)
½ kg spinach leaves - chopped
1 green chilli - chopped
1" piece ginger - chopped

OTHER INGREDIENTS FOR THE GRAVY
2 onions, 2 tomatoes, 2 laung (cloves) - grind together
4 tbsp oil, 1 tsp dhania powder, ½ tsp red chilli powder
¼ tsp garam masala, salt to taste

TADKA/TEMPERING
1 tbsp desi ghee
1" piece ginger - cut into match sticks
1 green chilli - slit lengthways
½ tsp red chilli powder

1. To prepare koftas, spread ¾ tbsp curd on each slice of bread to wet it. After spreading curd on both sides of bread, keep aside for a minute.
2. Mash the paneer well. Add baking powder, green chillies and coriander.
3. Mash the bread slices well and mix with the paneer. Add salt, pepper and red chilli powder to taste.
4. Add maida in the end. Mix well.
5. Make balls and stuff a piece of cashew in the centre.
6. Deep fry 4-5 pieces at a time, in medium hot oil and keep koftas aside.

contd...

7. To prepare the gravy, wash palak leaves and chop roughly. Put leaves with a green chilli and ginger in a pan and cook covered for 3-4 minutes after it boils. Remove from fire. Cool.

8. After the spinach cools, blend to a paste and keep aside.

9. Grind onions, tomatoes and 2 laung to a paste.

10. Heat 4 tbsp oil. Add the onion - tomato paste and cook stirring till dry.

11. Add masalas - dhania powder, red chilli powder, amchoor and salt to taste. Bhuno further for 1-2 minutes on low flame, till oil separates.

12. Add the ground spinach and bhuno for 2-3 minutes. Add ½ cup water to make a thin green gravy and bhuno for 5-7 minutes.

13. At serving time heat the spinach gravy and add the kofta. Stir gently on low flame for 1-2 minutes till the koftas are heated through. Remove from fire and transfer to a serving dish.

14. For the tadka, heat 1 tbsp desi ghee and add the ginger. When it turns brownish, shut off the flame. Add green chillies. Add red chilli powder and immediately pour the oil on the koftas in the serving dish. Mix lightly. Serve.

Baingan Di Kachri

Crisp brinjal slices coated with wheat flour.

Serves 4

1 medium round baingan (brinjal) - washed & cut into thin slices (15 slices)
1 tsp kuti laal mirch (red chilli flakes)
4-5 tbsp atta (whole wheat flour)
3-4 tbsp oil for shallow frying

1. Sprinkle 1½ tsp salt on brinjal slices, leave to sweat for 15-20 minutes. Drain out water. Pat dry.
2. Spread them on a plate. Sprinkle red chilli flakes and some atta on the slices. Overturn the slices and sprinkle more red chilli flakes and atta on the other side too. Keep aside till serving time.
3. At the time of serving, heat 3-4 tbsp oil in a frying pan or a tawa.
4. Fry 4-5 baingan slices at a time till crisp on both sides. Turn with the help of a chimta (tongs) or a knife to brown both sides.

Saabut Gobhi

Serves 4

2 very small whole cauliflowers, 4 tbsp oil

MASALA

3 onions - sliced finely, 3 tomatoes - roughly chopped, 1" ginger - chopped
2 tbsp curd, ½ tsp gram masala, ½ tsp red chilli powder, ½ tsp amchoor
salt to taste, ¼ cup boiled peas - to garnish

1. Remove stem of cauliflowers. Boil 5-6 cups water with 2 tsp salt. Put the whole cauliflowers in it and leave in hot water for 10 minutes. Remove from water and wash. Wipe dry with a towel.
2. Heat 5-6 tbsp oil in a large flat kadhai. Put both cauliflowers with flower side down in oil. Cover and cook on medium flame, stirring occasionally till the cauliflowers turn golden and get cooked. Remove from oil. Keep aside.
3. To prepare masala, grind onions to a paste.

4. Heat ½ tbsp oil in a clean kadhai. Add the chopped tomatoes and ginger. Cook for 4-5 minutes till soft. Cool. Grind tomatoes to a paste.
6. Heat 3 tbsp oil in a kadahi. Add onion paste, cook till brown.
7. Add tomato paste. Cook for 3-4 minutes on low flame till oil seperates.
8. Add well beaten curd. Cook till masala turns reddish again.
9. Add chilli powder, amchoor, garam masala & salt. Cook for1 minute.
10. Add 2-3 tbsp water to get a thick, dry masala. Boil. Cook for 1 minute on low flame. Remove from fire.
11. Insert a little masala in-between the florets of the fried cauliflower, especially from the backside.
12. To serve, arrange the cauliflowers on a platter. Add 3-4 tbsp water to the masala to make it a masala gravy. Boil. Pour over the arranged cauliflowers. Heat in a microwave or a preheated oven.

OR

Heat the cauliflower in a kadhai in 1 tbsp oil at the time of serving. Heat the masala separately by adding 2-3 tbsp water to get a thick masala gravy. Arrange the heated cauliflowers on a serving platter. Pour the hot masala gravy over it.
13. Sprinkle some boiled peas on it.

Pindi Chhole

Picture on facing page   *Serves 4*

PRESSURE COOK TOGETHER

1 cup channa kabuli (Bengal gram), 2 tbsp channe ki dal (split gram)
2 moti illaichi (big cardamoms), 1" stick dalchini (cinnamon)
2 tsp tea leaves tied in a muslin cloth or 2 tea bags

MASALA

2 onions - chopped finely
1½ tsp anaardana (pomegranate seeds) powder
1 big tomato - chopped finely
1" piece ginger - chopped finely
1 green chilli - chopped finely
½ tsp garam masala, 1 tsp dhania powder
1 tsp channa masala
salt & red chilli powder to taste

Bhature : Recipe on page 87, Pindi Chhole ➢

1. Soak channa and channe ki dal overnight or for 6-8 hours in a pressure cooker. Next morning, discard water. Wash channas with fresh water and add moti illaichi, dalchini, tea leaves, ¼ tsp soda and enough water to cover the channas nicely.
2. Pressure cook all the ingredients together to give one whistle. After the first whistle, keep on low flame for about 20-25 minutes. Keep aside.
3. Heat 4 tbsp oil. Add onions. Saute till transparent. Add anaardana powder. Cook stirring till onions turn dark brown. (Do not burn them).
4. Add chopped tomatoes, ginger and green chill. Stir fry for 3-4 minutes.
5. Add dhania powder, chilli powder & garam masala. Mash and stir fry tomatoes occasionally till they turn brownish in colour and oil separates.
6. Strain channas, reserving the liquid. Remove tea bag from the boiled channas and add to the onion-tomato masala. Mix well. Add salt. Stir fry gently for 5-7 minutes.
7. Add channa masala and salt. Add the channa liquid. Cook for 15-20 minutes on medium heat till the liquid dries up a little.
8. Serve garnished with onion rings, green chillies and tomato wedges.

Lahori Malai Kofte

Serves 6

150 gms paneer (cottage cheese) - grated
2 small boiled potatoes - grated
2 tbsp maida
½ tsp garam masala
½ tsp red chilli powder
¾ tsp salt, or to taste
2-3 tbsp maida (plain flour) - to coat

FILLING

½ onion - very finely chopped
½" tsp piece ginger - very finely chopped
4-5 kajus (cashews) - chopped finely
¼ tsp salt
¼ tsp red chilli powder
¼ tsp garam masala

GRAVY
a few strands kesar (saffron)
3 big onions
1½" piece ginger
2 dry, red chillies
2 tej patta (bay leaf)
4-5 chhoti illaichi (green cardamoms)
4 tbsp kaju (cashewnuts) - powdered
½ cup fresh thin malai - beaten with a fork or churned in the mixi for a second
3 tbsp desi ghee
½ tsp garam masala,¾ tsp red chilli powder, 1½ tsp salt, or to taste
1 tbsp kasoori methi (dry fenugreek leaves)
1½ cups milk mixed with 2 cups water

1.   To prepare the koftas, mix grated paneer, potatoes, red chilli powder, salt, garam masala and 2 tbsp maida.
2.   Mix well till the mixture is smooth. Make 12 balls.
3.   For filling, heat 2 tsp ghee. Add onions and ginger. Fry till golden brown. Add kaju, salt, garam masala and chilli powder. Remove from fire.

4. Flatten each ball of paneer mixture, put 1 tsp of onion filling in each ball. Form a ball again. Roll each ball in maida. Dust to remove excess maida.
5. Deep fry 1- 2 koftas at a time in medium hot oil. Keep aside.
6. To prepare the gravy, soak kesar in 1 tbsp warm water.
7. Grind onions, ginger & dry red chilli to a fine paste. Heat 2 tbsp ghee in a heavy bottomed kadhai and add the onion paste.
8. Add tej patta and chhoti illaichi. Cook on low flame for about 10-15 minutes till onions turn light brown and ghee separates.
9. Add masalas - garam masala, red chilli powder and salt.
10. Add malai. Cook for 3-4 minutes till masala turns brown again.
11. Add kaju powder. Cook for ½ minute.
12. Add milk mixed with water, to make a gravy. Boil. Simmer on low flame for 5 minutes.
13. Add kasoori methi. Discard bay leaves from the gravy.
14. Add kesar, keeping aside a little for garnishing.
15. To serve, boil gravy. Add koftas. Keep on low heat for ½ a minute. Serve immediately, sprinkled with cream and dotted with soaked kesar.

Paneer Makhani

Serves 4

250 gm paneer - cut into 1" cubes
3 tbsp desi ghee or butter
½ tsp jeera (cumin seeds)
4-5 flakes garlic - crushed
1 tbsp kasoori methi (dried fenugreek leaves)
1 tsp tomato ketchup
½ tsp garam masala, 2 tsp dhania powder
1 tsp salt, or to taste, ½ tsp red chilli powder
½ cup water
½ cup milk
½ cup cream (optional)

BOIL TOGETHER AND THEN GRIND TO A PASTE
5-6 large (500 gm) tomatoes - chopped roughly
2 green chillies - chopped, 1" piece ginger - chopped
¾ cup water

1. Boil tomatoes, green chillies and ginger for 5 minutes on low heat or till water is almost dry. Cool. Grind to a smooth puree.
2. Melt ghee or butter in a kadhai. Reduce heat. Add jeera. When it turns golden, add garlic.
3. When garlic starts to change colour add tomato puree. Cook till dry.
4. Add kasoori methi and tomato ketchup.
5. Add masalas - dhania powder, garam masala, salt and red chilli powder. Mix well for a few seconds. Cook till oil separates.
6. Add water. Boil. Simmer on low heat for 4-5 minutes. Reduce heat.
7. Mash 2-3 cubes of paneer and add to the gravy. Add the paneer cubes.
8. Keep aside to cool till serving time.
9. At serving time, add enough milk to the cold paneer masala to get a thick curry, mix gently. (Remember to add milk only after the masala turns cold, to prevent the milk from curdling. After adding milk, heat curry on low heat.)
10. Heat on low heat, stirring continuously till just about to boil.
11. Add cream, keeping the heat very low and stirring continuously. Remove from fire immediately. Serve with paranthas.

Matar Khumb Curry

Serves 6-8

1 packet (200 gm) mushrooms (khumb) - trim stalks & cut into 4 pieces
1 cup peas (shelled)
4 tbsp oil
2 moti illaichi (black cardamoms), 2 laung (cloves)
2 tsp salt, or to taste
2 tsp dhania powder
¼ tsp each - red chilli powder, garam masala, haldi

GRIND TOGETHER TO A PUREE
3 tomatoes
1 green chilli

GRIND TOGETHER TO A PASTE
1 large onion
6-8 flakes garlic, 1" piece ginger

1. Heat oil. Add moti illaichi and laung. Wait for 1 minute.
2. Add onion-garlic-ginger paste. Cook stirring continuously till light brown. Remove from fire.
3. Add masalas - salt, dhania powder, red chilli powder, garam masala and haldi.
4. Return to low heat and cook for a few seconds. Add 1 tbsp water.
5. Add the tomato-green chilli puree. Cook till dry and oil separates.
6. Add mushrooms and peas. Stir fry for 5 minutes. Add 1-2 tbsp water if required.
7. Add 2 cups water. Cook on low medium heat for about 15 minutes till peas turn soft and oil separates.
8. Serve curry with rice or chappatis.

Sarson Da Saag

Picture on page 103 *Serves 6*

1 bundle (1 kg) sarson (green mustard)
250 gm spinach or baathoo
2 shalgam (turnips) - peeled and chopped, optional
3-4 flakes garlic - finely chopped, optional
2" piece ginger - finely chopped
1 green chilli - chopped
¾ tsp salt, or to taste
2 tbsp makki ka atta (maize flour)
1½ tsp powdered gur (jaggery)

TADKA/TEMPERING
3 tbsp desi ghee
2 green chillies - finely chopped
1" piece ginger - finely chopped
½ tsp red chilli powder

Chicken Lollipops : Recipe on page 80 ➤

Punjabi Cooking

1. Wash and clean mustard leaves. First remove the leaves and then peel the stems, starting from the lower end and chop them finely. (Peel stems the way you string green beans). The addition of stems to the saag makes it tastier but it is important to peel the stems from the lower ends. The upper tender portion may just be chopped. Chop the spinach or baathoo leaves and mix with sarson.
2. Put chopped greens with ½ cup water in a pan.
3. Chop garlic, ginger and green chilli very finely and add to the saag, add shalgam if you wish. Add salt & put it on fire & let it start heating.
4. The saag will start going down. Cover and let it cook on medium fire for 15-20 minutes. Remove from fire, cool.
5. Grind to a rough paste. Do not grind too much.
6. Add makki ka atta to the saag and cook for 15 minutes on low heat.
7. At serving time, heat pure ghee. Reduce heat and add ginger & green chillies. Cook till ginger changes colour. Remove from fire and add red chilli powder. Add ghee to the hot saag and mix lightly. Serve hot.
8. Serve with fresh home made butter and makki-di-roti.

Note: Fresh saag should have tender leaves and tender stems (gandal).

Paneer Taka-Tak

Serves 4

300 gms paneer (cottage cheese) slab - cut into 1" thick rectangle of size -
8" x 3" approx. (get the paneer block cut horizontally when purchasing paneer)
2 capsicums
2 onions
1 firm tomato
1 cup (200 gms) curd of full cream milk - hang in a cloth for 15 minutes
¾ tsp salt, ½ tsp red chilli powder
¼ tsp orange red colour

DRY MASALA
5-6 chhoti illaichi (green cardamoms)
3-4 sticks dalchini (cinnamon)
8-10 laung (cloves)
1 tsp ajwain (carom seeds)

1. Grind chhoti illaichi, laung, dalchini and ajwain together. Keep aside.
2. Hang the curd in a fine muslin cloth for 15 minutes.
3. Add salt, chilli powder and enough colour to give the curd a bright orange colour.
4. Cover the paneer slab with this curd and keep in a greased wire rack or grill for atleast 15-20 minutes.
5. Heat the oven to 180°C. Keep the paneer which is marinated in curd in a preheated oven for 10-15 minutes or till the curd dries up and forms a coating. Keep a piece of aluminium foil beneath the wire rack to collect the drippings of the marinade.
6. Turn the paneer carefully when it appears dry.
7. Keep it in the oven for 5-7 minutes if it is wet on the other side.
8. Remove from the oven and keep aside.
9. Cut capsicums into 8 pieces to get 1" pieces of capsicum. Cut onion into four pieces and separate the onion leaves. Cut tomatoes into 8 pieces. Remove pulp.
10. Heat 1½ tbsp oil in a non-stick pan or a tawa. Add 1 tsp of the prepared dry masala.

contd...

11. Immediately put the slab of paneer. Cook on low heat for 1 minute. Do not let it turn black.
12. Turn the slab again. Remove from pan. Cut the paneer slab into 1" diagonal pieces.
13. At serving time, heat 2 tbsp oil in the pan, add 1 tsp dry masala powder, add the capsicum & onions immediately. Cook for 2-3 minutes. Add tomatoes, sprinkle ½ tsp salt on the vegetables. Mix well.
14. Add the paneer cubes and stir till paneer is heated through and turns soft. Serve.

Punj Rattani Dal

A combination of five lentils is used to prepare this dal delicacy.

Serves 4

FIVE DALS

(WASH ALL DALS AND SOAK TOGETHER FOR 2 HOURS)

¼ cup saboot moong dal (green)
¼ cup saboot masoor dal (brown)
¼ cup saboot urad dal (black)
¼ cup channa dal (yellow)
¼ cup tur dal (yellow)

OTHER INGREDIENTS

2 tbsp ghee
1 tsp shah jeera (black cumin seeds)
½ onion - chopped
2 tsp coriander powder, ½ tsp red chilli powder
½ tsp haldi, 1½ tsp salt, or to taste

TEMPERING
4 tbsp white butter or desi ghee
1 tomato - chopped finely, ½ cup yoghurt - beat well till smooth
½ tsp garam masala
seeds of 1 moti illaichi - crushed on a chakla, ½ tsp red chilli powder

1. Heat ghee in a heavy bottomed pan. Add shah jeera and saute over medium heat until they begin to crackle.
2. Add onion, saute until light brown.
3. Drain the dals and add to onion. Bhuno for 4-5 minutes on low heat.
4. Add 5 cups water & bring to a boil. Reduce heat & remove scum.
5. Add coriander powder, red chilli, haldi and salt, cover and simmer for about ½ hour, until lentils are done.
6. To prepare the tempering, melt butter or ghee in a kadhai, add tomatoes, yoghurt and garam masala, bhuno over medium heat until the fat leaves the sides. Add crushed seeds of moti illaichi. Stir for a few seconds. Add red chilli powder.
7. Add the cooked lentils and stir for 3-4 minutes. Remove to a bowl, garnish with some chopped coriander and serve hot.

Dal Makhani (Maanh Sabat)

Serves 6

1 cup urad saboot (whole black beans)
2 tbsp channe ki dal (split gram dal)
2 tbsp rajmah (kidney beans) - soaked for at least 6 hours or overnight, optional
1 tbsp ghee or oil
5 cups of water, 1½ tsp salt
2 dry whole red chillies, preferably Kashmiri red chillies
1" piece ginger
4 flakes garlic (optional)
4 tomatoes - pureed in a grinder
1 tbsp kasoori methi (dry fenugreek leaves), 1 tbsp tomato ketchup
3 tbsp ghee or oil
2 tsp dhania (coriander) powder, ½ tsp garam masala
2 tbsp butter
¼ cup fresh malai, beaten well and mixed with ¼ cup milk to make it ½ cup or
½ cup fresh cream

1. Clean, wash dals. If you want to add rajmah, soak both dals and rajmah together in a pressure cooker for 6 hours or overnight.
2. Grind ginger and garlic together to a paste.
3. Discard water from the soaked dals and add 6 cups of fresh water.
4. Pressure cook both dals and rajmah with 1 tbsp ghee, salt, half of the ginger-garlic paste & the dry, red chillies. Keep the left over paste aside.
5. After the first whistle, keep on low flame for 40 minutes. Remove from fire. After the pressure drops, mash the hot dal a little. Keep aside.
6. Heat ghee. Add tomatoes pureed in a grinder. Cook until thick & dry.
7. Add the left over ginger-garlic paste, garam masala and coriander powder. Cook until ghee separates.
8. Add kasoori methi and tomato ketchup. Cook further for 1-2 minutes.
9. Add this tomato mixture to the boiled dal.
10. Add butter. Simmer on low flame for 20-25 minutes, stirring & mashing the dal occasionally with a kadchhi against the sides of the cooker.
11. Add beaten malai mixed with milk or cream. Mix very well with a kadcchi. Simmer for 15-20 minutes more, to get the right colour and smoothness. Remove from fire. Serve hot.

Achaari Baingans

Serves 4

250 gm chhote baingan (brinjals)
3 tbsp oil
½ tsp kalonji, ½ tsp sarson, ¼ tsp methi dana
2-3 red chillies
2 tbsp curry leaves
3 tbsp tamarind pulp (soak a marble size ball of imli in ½ cup warm water and
squeeze to extract pulp)
1 tsp sugar, or to taste

GRIND TO A PASTE
3-4 flakes garlic (1 tsp chopped)
1" piece ginger
1 small onion
2 tsp saunf (fennel)
½ tsp each of garam masala, haldi & red chilli powder
1 tsp dhania powder, 1 tsp amchoor powder, 1½ tsp salt

1. Wash baingans and give two cuts crossing each other, more than half way, almost till the end, keeping the end intact. Keep aside.
2. Grind all ingredients together with 2 tbsp water.
3. Fill the brinjals nicely with the masala, pushing it down with a knife.
4. Heat 3 tbsp oil in a big, heavy bottomed kadhai. Add kalonji, sarson and methi dana.
5. Reduce heat. Add dry red chillies and curry leaves.
6. When methi dana turns golden, add baingans. Stir to mix well. Add the left over masala, if any. Cover and cook, spreading them in the kadhai and stirring occasionally, for 15 minutes or till done. Do not stir frequently, otherwise they might break.
7. Add the sugar and tamarind pulp. Mix. Serve hot.

Khaja Aloo

Potatoes are simmered in a delicious, yellow masala. Curd and cashews form the base of this masala. Black cumin lends it's royal flavour to the potatoes.

Serves 8-10

4 potatoes
1 tsp shah jeera (black cumin)
1 tej patta (bay leaf)
2 onions - chopped
¼ tsp haldi (turmeric)
½ tsp garam masala
2 tbsp chopped coriander
½ cup curd (yogurt) - whisked to make it smooth
oil for frying plus 4 tbsp oil

GRIND TO A PASTE
4 tbsp cashews - soaked in ¼ cup water
1 tbsp chopped ginger
1 tsp chopped garlic

1. Wash potatoes and peel. Cut potatoes into 1" pieces.
2. Fry the potatoes to a deep golden brown and keep aside.
3. Grind cashews, ginger and garlic to a paste in a small coffee or spice grinder. Keep cashew paste aside.
4. Heat 4 tbsp oil in a heavy bottomed pan. Add shah jeera and tej patta. Wait for 30 seconds till jeera stops spluttering.
5. Add onions and cook on low heat till onions turn soft but do not let them turn brown. Add haldi and garam masala. Stir to mix well.
6. Add yogurt and stir fry on low heat till water evaporates. Cook till dry.
7. Add cashew paste. Cook for 1 minute.
8. Add about 1 cup water to get a gravy. Boil and simmer for 2-3 minutes.
9. Add the fried potatoes and chopped coriander to the gravy and simmer on low heat.
10. Cook on low heat till gravy gets thick and coats the potatoes. Serve hot with rotis or paranthas.

SNACKS

Besan Di Murgi

Serves 3-4

400 gms chicken - cut into pieces or 6 legs (drumsticks)
¾ cup milk
1 tsp red chilli powder, ¾ tsp salt

GRIND TOGETHER TO A PASTE
½" piece ginger
2-3 flakes garlic
2 saboot kali mirch (peppercorns)
2 laung (cloves)
2 chhoti illaichi (green cardamoms)
1 tsp jeera (cumin seeds)
2 tsp saboot dhania (coriander seeds)
¾" stick dalchini
¾ tsp saunf (fennel)

COATING
8 tbsp besan, 6 tbsp curd
1 tbsp chopped fresh dhania
½ tsp salt, ¼ tsp red chilli powder
¼ tsp ajwain (carom seeds)

1. Grind together ginger, garlic along with all the saboot masalas. Use a little water if required. Keep the ground masala aside.
2. Mix together ¾ cup milk with ¼ cup water. Heat and bring to a boil.
3. Add the above ground masala, 1 tsp red chilli powder and ¾ tsp salt.
4. Add chicken also to the milk. Give 1-2 boils. Cover and lower heat. Cook for 8-10 minutes or till chicken is tender. Increase heat and cook till completely dry. Remove from fire. Cool.
5. To the cooked chicken add all the coating ingredients. Mix well.
6. Heat oil and fry 2-3 pieces at a time to a golden brown colour.
7. Serve hot with mint chutney, onion rings and lemon wedges

Note: Chops/Ribs can also be cooked in this manner. Only at stage 4, after 1-2 boils, give 2-3 whistles in a pressure cooker to ensure that the ribs get tender.

Punjabi Aloo Tikki

Makes 10   *Picture on page 75*

½ kg (6 medium) potatoes - boiled and mashed
2 tbsp cornflour
1 tsp salt
ghee or oil for shallow frying

FILLING
1/3 cup channa dal (Bengal gram)
½ tsp jeera (cumin seed)
½" piece ginger - finely chopped
salt to taste
2 green chillies - finely chopped
½ tsp red chillies
½ tsp chaat masala
½ tsp garam masala
1 tbsp coriander leaves - chopped

Punjabi Cooking

1. Soak channe ki dal for 3-4 hours.
2. Heat 1 tbsp oil or ghee in a kadhai. Add jeera, let it turn golden. Add chopped green chillies, red chillies and salt.
3. Drain dal and add to the kadhai. Cover and let it cook on low heat till it turns soft and gets cooked. Sprinkle some water while it is being cooked.
4. Cook dal till soft and dry. Add chaat masala, garam masala and chopped coriander leaves. Remove from fire and keep aside to cool.
5. Boil, peel and mash potatoes. Add 2 tbsp cornflour and 1 tsp salt.
6. Take a ball of mashed potatoes and oil palm slightly. Make a shallow cup with the ball of mashed potatoes. Place a tbsp of dal filling in centre and seal well to form a ball. Flatten the ball.
7. Heat oil on a tawa or a frying pan. Shallow fry 2-3 tikkis at a time till golden and crisp on both sides. Once done, shift to the sides and put fresh ones in the centre. This way the tikkis turn really crisp. Serve hot with imli and poodina chutney.

Punjabi Aloo Tikki : Recipe on page 73 ➢

Amritsari Machhi

Delicious fried fish with the flavour of ajwain.

Picture on page 2   *Serves 5-6*

800 gms fish (10-12 pieces), preferably boneless, generally Sole fish is used but
any fish can be used
2 tbsp plus 6 tbsp besan (gram flour)
some chaat masala for sprinkling on top
oil for frying

MARINADE
3 tsp ajwain (carom seeds)
3 tsp garlic paste
3 tsp ginger paste
2½ tsp salt
3 tsp red chilli powder
2 tsp garam masala
8-10 tbsp lemon juice

1. Rub fish with 1 tsp salt and 2 tbsp besan. Keep aside for 10 minutes. Wash well to remove all smell.
2. Mix together all ingredients of the marinade.
3. Rub this marinade on the fish and leave the fish to marinate for 2-3 hours in the fridge.
4. At the time of serving, sprinkle 6 tbsp besan on fish and rub it so that the besan lightly coats the fish.
5. Deep fry to a golden brown colour till the fish is cooked and crisp.
6. Sprinkle chaat masala and serve hot garnished with onion rings, lemon wedges and sprigs of coriander or mint.

Note:

1. A few drops of colour (orange red) can be added to the marinade for a tandoori colour.
2. For a different flavour 1-1½ tsp kasoori methi (dry fenugreek leaves) can be added in the marinade.

Mewa Kebab

Rich seekh kebabs for special occasions.

Serves 4 - 5

½ kg (500 gm) keema (chicken mince)
1 cup dry bread crumbs, 1 tsp oil, 1 tbsp cornflour
½ tsp garam masala, ½ tsp salt
1 tsp magaz (watermelon seeds), 1 tbsp chironji (sunflower seeds)

GRIND TOGETHER

1" piece ginger, 6-8 flakes garlic, 2 green chillies, ¼ cup green coriander
1½ tbsp kaju (cashewnuts), 6 badam (almonds) - blanched and peeled
5 kishmish (raisins), ½ tsp whole pista (pistachio)
¼ tsp jaiphal (nutmeg), ¼ tsp javetri (mace)
½ tbsp kachri powder

BASTING (POURING)

2 tbsp melted butter or oil

1. Wash the mince and squeeze out all the excess water. Grind the mince twice till smooth.
2. Roast magaz and chironji on a hot tawa. Cool.
3. Grind ginger, garlic, green chillies, coriander, kaju, badam, kishmish, pista, jaiphal, javetri, kachri and roasted chironji and magaz in a grinder. Remove from grinder to a bowl.
4. Add bread crumbs, cornflour, garam masala, oil, salt and chicken mince. Mix well and marinate in the refrigerator for 4-5 hours.
5. Heat an electric oven at 180°C or a gas tandoor on moderate heat.
6. Take a big ball of the mince mixture and hold a well greased hot skewer carefully in the other hand. Press the mince on to a hot skewer. The mince will immediately stick to the hot skewer. If the skewers are cold the mince will not stick. Make one big seekh on the skewer. Repeat with the left over mince on all the other skewers.
7. Place the skewers in the hot oven or tandoor. Cook for 10-15 minutes or till done, rotating the skewers. When the seekhs get cooked, gently remove the kebab from the skewers with the help of a cloth. Cut each into 1" pieces to serve.

Chicken Lollipops

A delicious snack made from chicken wings. The lollipops look like mini dumb bells. Remember to cover the end of the bone of the lollipops with a piece of aluminium foil.

Picture on page 57   Serves 3-4

600 gms lollipops
oil for frying

MIX TOGETHER
1½ tsp ginger paste
1½ tsp garlic paste
1 tsp salt
1½ tsp Kashmiri red chilli powder (degi mirch)
2 tsp amchoor powder
1 tsp garam masala
a pinch of tandoori red colour
4 tbsp maida (plain flour)

1. Mix all the ingredients together.
2. Mix the lollipops in the mixture and let them marinate for 3-4 hours in the refrigerator.
3. At the time of serving, shape each piece to give them a neat look.
4. Shallow fry in a pan in 5-6 tbsp oil, turning sides or deep fry a few at a time till tender and crisp. If you shallow fry, keep the pan covered so that the chicken gets done while frying.
5. Drain on a paper napkin.
6. Serve on a bed of onion rings along with lemon wedges.

Fried Fish

Punjabis love and enjoy fried and heavy food. Fried fish is a great favourite of the Punjabis and is made in many different ways. It is an excellent snack and is also served with the main meal.

Serves 4

600 gms fish (8 pieces) - preferably boneless and skinless

GRIND TO A PASTE
7-8 flakes garlic
5-6 green chillies
1" piece ginger
1 cup chopped fresh coriander leaves
4-5 tbsp lemon juice
2 tsp salt

COATING
6 tbsp maida (flour)
½ tsp salt, ½ tsp red chilli powder

1 egg - beaten lightly
oil for frying

1. Rub fish with a little salt & lemon juice or besan. Wash well and pat dry.
2. Grind together garlic, chillies and ginger, chopped coriander, lemon juice and salt to a paste.
3. Rub the paste well on the fish. Leave the fish to marinate for 2-3 hours in the refrigerator.
4. Mix maida with salt and red chilli powder.
5. Lightly beat the egg and keep aside.
6. Heat oil for frying. Coat fish pieces with maida, dip in beaten egg and fry to a golden brown colour.
7. Serve hot with mint chutney or tomato sauce.

Note:

1. If fish is fried in mustard oil it has a better flavour and taste.
2. Large prawns can also be cooked in this way.

Achaari Paneer Tikka

Pickle flavoured masala paneer tikka.

Picture on page 1   *Makes* 12

400 gms paneer - cut into 1½" rectangles of ¾" thickness
2 tsp ginger-garlic paste
1 tsp cornflour, 1 cup curd - hang in a muslin cloth for ½ hour
2 tbsp oil
½ tsp haldi (turmeric) powder, 1 tsp amchoor (dried mango powder)
1 tsp dhania powder, ½ tsp garam masala, 1 tsp salt or to taste, ½ tsp sugar
1 onion - chopped finely, 2 green chillies - chopped
some chaat masala to sprinkle

ACHAARI MASALA
1 tbsp saunf (aniseeds)
½ tsp rai (mustard seeds)
a pinch of methi daana (fenugreek seeds)
½ tsp kalonji (onion seeds)
½ tsp jeera (cumin seeds)

1. Collect seeds of achaari masala- saunf, rai, methi daana, kalonji and jeera together.
3. Heat 2 tbsp oil. Add the collected seeds together to the hot oil. Let saunf change colour.
4. Add onions and chopped green chillies. Cook till onions turn golden brown.
5. Reduce heat. Add haldi, amchoor, dhania powder, garam masala, salt and sugar. Mix. Remove from fire.
6. Beat curd till smooth. Add garlic-ginger paste and cornflour. Add the onion masala also to the curd.
7. Add the paneer cubes to the curd. Marinate till serving time.
8. At serving time, rub oil generously over the grill of the oven or wire rack of a gas tandoor. Place paneer on the greased wire rack or grill of the oven.
9. Heat an oven to 180°C or a gas tandoor on moderate flame. Grill paneer for 15 minutes. Spoon some oil or melted butter on the paneer pieces in the oven or tandoor and grill further for 5 minutes. Serve hot sprinkled with chaat masala.

ROTI & CHAAWAL

Bhature

Makes 8   *Picture on page 47*

2 cups maida (plain flour)
1 cup suji (semolina)
½ tsp soda-bicarb, ½ tsp salt
½ tsp sugar, ½ cup sour curd
oil for deep frying

1.   Soak suji in water, which is just enough to cover it. Keep aside for 10 minutes.
2.   Sift salt, soda and maida in a paraat. Add sugar, suji and curd.
3.   Knead with enough warm water to make a dough of rolling consistency.
4.   Knead again with greased hands till the dough is smooth.
5.   Brush the dough with oil. Keep the dough in a greased polythene and keep it in a warm place for 3-4 hours.
6.   Make 8-10 balls. Roll each ball to an oblong shape.
7.   Deep fry in hot oil and serve hot with Pindi chhole.

Makki Di Roti

Picture on page 103   *Makes 6-7*

2 cups makki da atta (maize flour)
hot water - to knead
ghee for frying

1. Sieve the flour. Knead gently with hot water to a soft dough. Do not knead the dough too much in advance.
2. Tear an old polythene bag into two halves. Keep one piece of polythene on the chakla (rolling platform). Put a ball of the kneaded dough on the polythene. Cover with the other piece of plastic, such that there is a plastic cover above and beneath the ball.
3. Roll carefully to a slightly thick roti.
4. Cook the roti on both sides on a tawa. Add some ghee and fry both sides on low flame.
5. Serve hot with sarson da saag.

Poodina Parantha

Makes 8

2 cups atta (whole wheat flour)
2 tbsp poodina (mint leaves), freshly chopped or dry
1 tsp ajwain (carom seeds)
2 tbsp ghee
½ tsp salt, ½ tsp red chilli powder

1. Mix atta with all ingredients except poodina. Add enough water to make a dough of rolling consistency. Cover and keep the dough aside for 30 minutes.
2. Make walnut sized balls. Roll out a little to make a thick chappati.
3. Spread 1 tsp ghee all over. Fold a little from the left and then right to meet in the centre. Fold the top and the bottom to now get a square.
4. Roll out to get a square parantha, but do not make it too thin. Sprinkle poodina. Press with the belan (rolling pin).
5. Cook on a tawa, frying on both sides till crisp and well browned.

Champae Waale Chaawal

Serves 4-5

300 gms mutton ribs (champae) - 4 pieces
1½ cups rice - washed and strained and kept in the strainer for 15 minutes after
washing (do not soak rice)
3 tbsp ghee, 3 tbsp oil
2-3 saboot kali mirch (black peppercorns)
1 moti illaichi (black cardamom)
2-3 laung (cloves), 1" dalchini (cinnamon)
1 tej patta (bay leaf)
2 medium onions - sliced
3 flakes garlic - chopped
¾" piece ginger - chopped
2 tomatoes - chopped
2½ tsp salt
1 tsp garam masala
1¼ tsp Kashmiri red chilli powder

GARNISH
1 egg - hard boiled and cut into 4 pieces lengthwise
some fresh coriander

1. Heat oil and ghee in a pressure cooker. Add saboot kali mirch, moti illaichi, laung, dalchini and tej patta. Fry for 1 minute.
2. Add sliced onions, garlic and ginger and fry till onions turn soft.
3. Add mutton, tomatoes, salt, garam masala powder and red chill powder. Fry for 8-10 minutes.
4. Add 1½ cups water and pressure cook to give 1 whistle. Keep on low heat for 20 minutes. Remove from fire. After the pressure drops, dry the water on fire.
5. Add washed rice. Fry for 1 minute. Add 3 cups water. Mix well.
6. Close the cooker and give 3 whistles.
7. When the pressure drops, check if rice is dry, (water is absorbed by the rice).
8. Fluff rice with a fork and serve hot garnished with fresh coriander and hard boiled egg wedges.

Amritsari Nan

Makes 6

2½ cups (250 gms) maida (plain flour), ½ tsp salt
½ cup hot milk, 1 tsp baking powder, ½ cup warm water (approx)
10 badaam (almonds) - skinned & cut into long thin pieces,1 tbsp kasoori methi

1. Heat milk and put it in a paraat or a large pan. Add baking powder to the hot milk. Mix well & keep aside for 1-2 minutes till it starts to bubble.
2. Sift maida and salt together. Add maida to the hot milk. Mix.
3. Knead to a dough with warm water. Keep in a warm place for 3 hours.
4. Make 6-8 balls. Roll out each ball to an oblong shape. Spread ghee all over. Fold one side (lengthways) a little, so as to overlap an inch of the nan. Press lightly on the joint with the belan (rolling pin).
5. Sprinkle some kasoori methi & almonds. Press with a rolling pin (belan). Pull one side of the nan to give it a pointed end like the nan.
6. Apply some water on the back side of nan. Stick in a hot gas tandoor.
7. Cook till nan is ready. Spread butter on the ready nan and serve hot.

Phirni : Recipe on page 102 ➢

Peethi Poori

Makes 12

1 cup atta (whole wheat flour)
1 tsp oil or melted ghee, ½ tsp salt
¼ cup urad dal - soaked for 2 hours and coarsely ground to get peethi
or ½ cup ready made dal ki peethi, 1 tsp suji (semolina)
½ tsp salt, 1 tsp kuti laal mirch (red chilli flakes), ¼ tsp ajwain (carom seeds)

1. Sift flour and ½ tsp salt together and rub in melted ghee or oil.
2. Knead to a little stiff dough with about ¾-1 cup water and set aside.
3. Mix peethi with ½ tsp salt, kuti laal mirch, ajwain and 1 tsp suji.
4. Divide dough into small balls and roll out the balls into small poories.
5. Spread 1 tsp full peethi on the rolled out poori with the spoon. The peethi is spread on the outside of the puri instead of stuffing it within.
6. Heat oil, drop the rolled poories gently into the oil **with the peethi side down in the oil,** so that the dal gets cooked in the hot oil.
7. Fry till golden brown and crisp. The peethi can be stuffed inside the poori also, if you like.

MITTHA

Pista Kesar Kulfi

Serves 6

1 kg (4 cups) full cream milk, a few strands of kesar (saffron)
¼ cup sugar, 2 tbsp cornflour
75 gms fresh khoya - grated & mashed slightly (¾ cup grated)
1 tbsp pista - very finely cut
1 tbsp almonds - very finely cut
3-4 crushed chhoti illaichi (green cardamoms)

1. Dissolve cornflour in 1 cup milk and keep aside.
2. Boil the rest of the milk with kesar in a kadhai till it is reduced to half in quantity, for about 25-30 minutes on medium fire, scraping the sides to get a real malaidar kulfi.
3. Add sugar and cornflour paste. Boil. Cook for 2-3 minutes more till the sugar is well dissolved.
4. Remove from fire. Cool slightly.
5. Add khoya, almonds, pista and crushed illaichi.
6. Fill the mixture in the kulfi moulds. Freeze for 6-8 hours or overnight.

Jalebi Te Rabri

Serves 8

JALEBI
1 cup maida (plain flour)
1 tbsp besan (gram flour)
¼ tsp (level) soda bicarb
½ tbsp oil
½ cup thick curd
¾ cup warm water
oil or ghee for frying

SYRUP
1¼ cups sugar, ¾ cup water
2-3 pinches orange-red colour

1. Sieve maida, besan and soda bi carb. Add curd and oil. Add enough warm water (about ¾ cup) to make a batter of a soft dropping consistency.

contd...

2. Beat batter well till smooth. Cover and keep aside for 30-40 minutes.
3. Heat oil or ghee in a frying pan till medium hot. Put the batter in a piping bag and make circles within circle, starting from the outside.
4. Reduce heat. Fry them golden brown on low heat on both sides, turning carefully with a pair of tongs (chimta). Remove from oil, drain excess oil and keep aside.
5. For the syrup, boil sugar, water and colour in a kadhai. After the first boil keep on low flame for 5-7 minutes till a stringy syrup is attained.
6. At serving time, dip 4-5 jalebis at a time in the hot syrup for 1 minute, take out and serve them hot with rabri.

RABRI

4 cups full cream milk
75 gm khoya - grated, (½ cup)
2 tbsp sugar
6-8 pistas - chopped
3 chhoti illaichi (green cardamoms) - powdered
rose petals or silver sheet (varq)

1. Boil milk in a heavy bottomed kadhai. Add khoya and sugar.
2. Simmer on low-medium heat for about 40-45 minutes, scraping the sides, till the quantity is reduced to almost half and the mixture turns thick with a thick pouring consistency. Remove from fire. The rabri turns thick on keeping.
3. Add some chopped pistas and cardamom powdered into the mixture.
4. Transfer to a serving dish and garnish with pistas and rose petals.
5. Chill and serve plain by itself or with jalebis or with some fruit.

Kesari Mitthe Chaawal

Serves 4

1 cup Basmati rice - must be soaked for 1 hour
a few strands of kesar (saffron)
1 cup sugar
3 tbsp desi ghee
4 chhoti illaichi (green cardamoms)
3 laung (cloves)
a small piece of fresh or dried coconut - cut into thin pieces, optional
1 tbsp kishmish (raisins) - soaked in water
6-8 badam (almonds) - blanched & shredded

1. Mix ¾ cup water and 1 cup sugar in a small pan. Add kesar. Keep on fire to boil. Stir in between. Remove from fire as soon as syrup boils. Keep aside.
2. Heat ghee in a big heavy bottomed pan. Reduce heat. Add chhoti illaichi and laung. Stir fry for a few seconds till illaichi changes colour.

3. Add coconut, almonds and kishmish. Stir till kishmish swells.
4. Discard water from soaked rice and add the rice to the ghee. Mix gently so that the rice grains do not break.
5. Add 1¼ cups water. Boil.
6. Reduce flame. Keep a tawa under the pan of rice as soon as it starts to boil to reduce the heat further.
7. Cook for about 10 minutes till the water gets absorbed.
8. Add the kesar waala sugar syrup. Mix lightly with a fork. Cover and cook further on low heat till rice is done and the syrup gets absorbed.
9. Serve after 10 minutes, so that the rice is fully done.

Phirni

Picture on page 93   *Serves 6*

3½ cups (700 gm) milk, ¼ cup basmati rice
¼ cup sugar plus 1 tbsp more, or to taste
4 almonds (badaam) - shredded, 5-6 green pistas (pistachio) - shredded
2 small silver leaves, optional, 2-3 chhoti illaichi (green cardamom) - powdered
1 drop kewra essence or 1 tsp ruh kewra, a few rose petals - to decorate

1. Soak rice for about an hour in a little water. Drain and grind with 4-5 tbsp of water to a very smooth paste. Mix rice paste with ½ cup milk and make it thinner. Keep aside.
2. Mix the rice paste with all the milk in a clean, heavy bottomed pan.
3. Cook on medium heat, stirring continuously and let it boil. Boil, stirring constantly for 2-3 minutes more to get a mixture of creamy consistency.
4. Add sugar and cardamom powder and mix well for a few seconds.
5. Remove from fire. Add ruh kewra or essence. Pour the mixture into 6 small silver or earthen bowls. Chill. Decorate each bowl with a silver leaf and a few shredded nuts and rose petals.

Sarsoon Da Saag : Recipe on page 56, Makki Di Roti : Recipe on page 88 ➢

Nita Mehta's BEST SELLERS (Non-Veg)

CHINESE Cookery

Tikka Seekh & Kebab

OVEN Recipes Non-Veg

BREAKFAST Non-Veg

ITALIAN
Non-Vegetarian

Favourite Recipes

MICROWAVE
Cookery

CONTINENTAL
Non-Vegetarian

MUGHLAI
Cooking

SNACKS
Non-Vegetarian

The Best of
CHICKEN Recipes

Favourite
NON-VEGETARIAN